I Wi

Jack Gabolinscy

Sue Dani

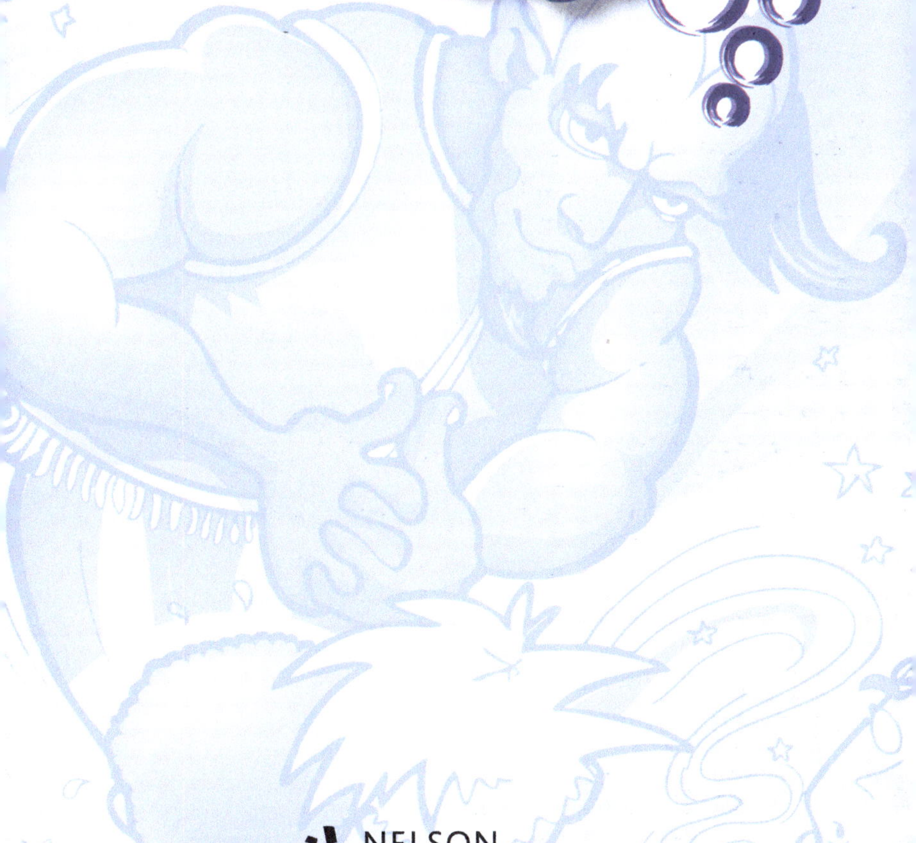

NELSON
CENGAGE Learning™

Australia • Brazil • Japan • Korea • Mexico • Singapore • Spain • United Kingdom • United States

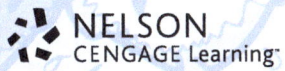

I Wish

Fast Forward
Gold Level 22

Text: Jack Gabolinscy
Illustrations: Sue Dani
Editor: Johanna Rohan
Design: Vonda Pestana
Series design: James Lowe
Production controller: Seona Galbally
Audio recordings: Juliet Hill, Picture Start
Spoken by: Matthew King and Abbe Holmes
Reprint: Siew Han Ong

Text © 2007 Cengage Learning Australia Pty Limited
Illustrations © 2007 Cengage Learning Australia Pty Limited

Copyright Notice
This Work is copyright. No part of this Work may be reproduced, stored in a retrieval system, or transmitted in any form or by any means without prior written permission of the Publisher. Except as permitted under the *Copyright Act 1968*, for example any fair dealing for the purposes of private study, research, criticism or review, subject to certain limitations. These limitations include: Restricting the copying to a maximum of one chapter or 10% of this book, whichever is greater; Providing an appropriate notice and warning with the copies of the Work disseminated; Taking all reasonable steps to limit access to these copies to people authorised to receive these copies; Ensuring you hold the appropriate Licences issued by the Copyright Agency Limited ("CAL"), supply a remuneration notice to CAL and pay any required fees

ISBN 978 0 17 012682 3
ISBN 978 0 17 012681 6 (set)

Cengage Learning Australia
Level 7, 80 Dorcas Street
South Melbourne, Victoria Australia 3205
Phone: 1300 790 853

Cengage Learning New Zealand
Unit 4B Rosedale Office Park
331 Rosedale Road, Albany, North Shore NZ 0632
Phone: 0800 449 725

For learning solutions, visit **cengage.com.au**

Printed in Australia by Ligare Pty Ltd
6 7 8 9 10 11 20 19 18 17 16

Evaluated in independent research by staff from the Department of Language, Literacy and Arts Education at the University of Melbourne.

Contents

Chapter 1 **A Holiday**   4
Chapter 2 **Across the Pacific**   9
Chapter 3 **A Bad Storm**   11
Chapter 4 **A Small Island**   14
Chapter 5 **A Big Bottle**   18

Chapter 1

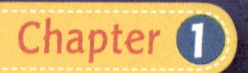

A HOLIDAY

Pele, Ron and Pete moaned as they walked to school.

"I hate school," moaned Pele. "I hate reading and writing."

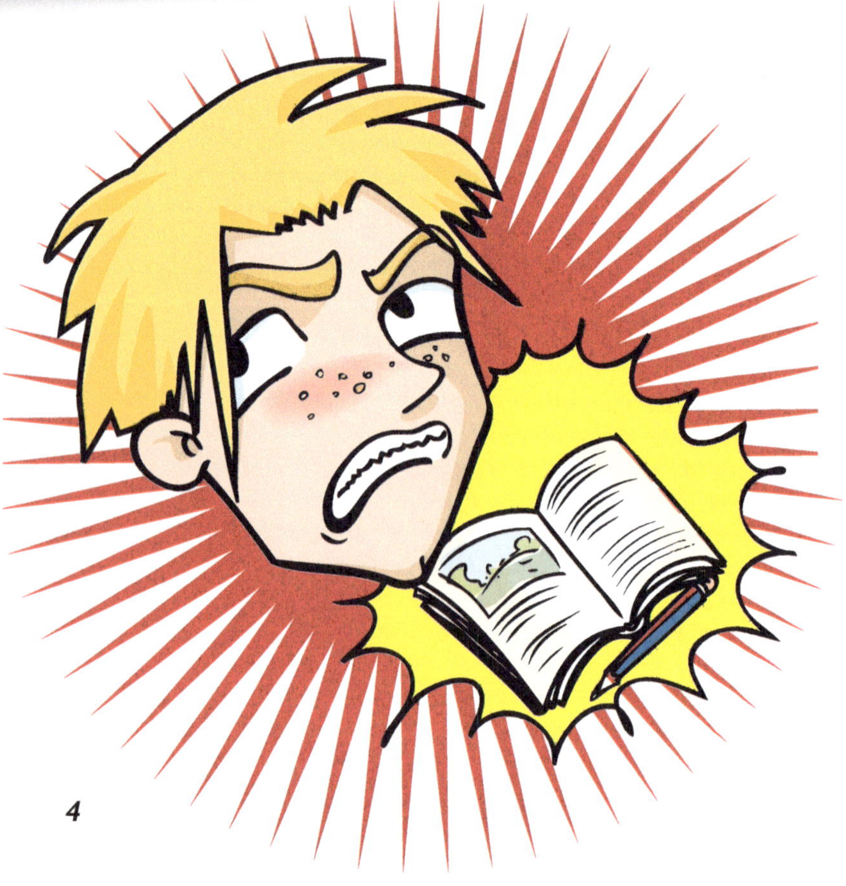

A Holiday

"Yeah," moaned Ron. "I hate all the subjects."

"Me too, dudes," agreed Pete.

"I'm tired of working so hard," complained Pele.

"I'm sick of being a slave," complained Ron.

"Dudes, school is like a bad smell," said Pete.

"Yeah," agreed Ron.
"At least we're on school holidays soon."

"Dudes, why don't we run away to the Pacific Ocean for our holidays?" said Pete.
"There are no schools there."

"How do we get there?" asked Pele.

"We can borrow my uncle's yacht," said Ron.
"He's not using it."

A Holiday

Pete held up a hand to his ear. "Listen, dudes," he said. "Freedom is calling. Let's go!"

The boys high-fived each other, and started to plan their holiday.

ACROSS THE PACIFIC

A week later, the three friends were sailing across the Pacific Ocean. Captain Pele steered the boat. "This is better than going to school!" he shouted.

Ron caught some fish. "Yeah, this is better than reading and writing," he yelled back.

I Wish

Pete just cooked the fish.
He sniffed the sea air and grinned.

Day after day, they sailed across
the Pacific Ocean.
There was no work, no school,
just the open sea
and the blue sky.
The three boys were so happy.

A BAD STORM

One day, the blue sky turned black.
The soft breeze turned into a wild wind.

Lightning flashed, and thunder crashed.
Big waves smashed into the boat.
It rocked and rolled on the stormy sea.

"I wish I was at school reading a book," moaned Pele.

"I wish I was writing a story," moaned Ron.

"I wish I was on dry land," cried Pete.

The boat bounced like a beach ball on the waves.
Suddenly, a huge wave smashed into it.
The boat rolled upside down.

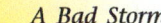
A Bad Storm

The boys climbed onto the bottom of the boat.
They thought the boat would sink and they were going to drown.
But then, just as quickly as it had started, the storm stopped and the Sun came out.

A SMALL ISLAND

The boys were happy when they saw
that they were near a tiny island.
They swam to the island.

There were coconut trees,
banana trees and pineapples growing
everywhere.
They liked the yellow sand
and the clear blue pools.

"Dudes, this is better than
reading a book!" smiled Pete.

A Small Island

The boys loved their island holiday. They spent their days swimming, fishing and laughing.

I Wish

But after a few days,
they grew tired of eating the same food
and doing the same things.

"I'm bored," said Pele.
"I'd sooner read fifty books
than eat one more coconut."

A Small Island

"I'm bored, too!" agreed Ron. "I'd sooner do one hundred maths problems than eat another pineapple."

"I'd rather be sailing back home," moaned Pete.

Chapter 5

A BIG BOTTLE

Pele watched a green spot bobbing up and down on the waves.
"What's that?" he asked Pete and Ron.

The three friends watched as the green spot came closer.
"It's a bottle," said Ron.
"I'm going to get it."

He brought it back and stood it
in the sand.
It was a very old, big, green bottle
with a big cork in it.
Ron tried to pull the cork out,
but it wouldn't come out.

Then Pele took the bottle
and pulled and pulled,
but still the cork wouldn't come out.

Then Pete had a turn.
He held the bottle with his feet.
He gripped the cork tightly
and pulled and pulled …

Suddenly, in a cloud of smoke,
the cork shot out of the bottle.
The boys looked up
and saw a giant genie
standing over them.

"Thank you!" the genie roared.
"You have saved my life.
For setting me free,
I will grant you one wish each.
What do you wish for?"
The genie turned to Pele.

A Big Bottle

I Wish

"I wish I was back at school,"
said Pele.
"I want to be in class reading a book."

There was a flash of lightning
and a clap of thunder,
and Pele was back at school reading.

"What is your wish?"
the genie asked Ron.

"I want the same as Pele,"
said Ron.
"I want to be back at school,
writing a story."

There was a flash of lightning
and a clap of thunder,
and Ron was back at school,
writing.

The genie looked down at Pete.
"What is your wish?" he asked.

Pete scratched his head,
but he couldn't think what to wish for.

I Wish

The genie was impatient.
"Come on!" he roared.
"I've been in that bottle for 2000 years.
Hurry up!
What's your wish?"

"I don't know …" said Pete.
"It's lonely without my friends.
Oh, I wish they were still here."

There were two flashes of lightning
and two claps of thunder …